A Book of Maps

Contents

FOREWORD

THIS set of maps tells a great deal about what could be called the embryology of the United States. The maps show the rate and the direction of thrust of land settlement in the United States, 1790 to 1900; they also suggest some of the political and economic developments that accompanied this great movement of population onto the American land.

For a number of years in teaching my classes in the history of the westward movement in the United States I used color slides made from the plates in the *Statistical Atlas of the Twelfth Census of the United States, 1900* that show the successive frontier lines. These maps are very useful but they also have limitations. Through 1860 the maps show only the eastern half of the United States. Moreover, they include too much data for satisfactory classroom use. Three years ago we began to redraw these maps so as to produce what we hoped would be more useful slides. All the successive frontier lines were to be shown on a projection of the whole area that was to become the continental United States and only a limited amount of political and economic data was to be included. In addition to showing the exfoliation of political boundaries and providing some data on exploration and transportation on or beyond the frontier line, we included material on the establishment and location of district land offices. The land office represents a nucleus of economic growth on the frontier. The opening of such an office meant that there was a demand for land in the area; the closing meant that most of the land in the district had been disposed of. The length of time that the office continued in existence was an indication of the attractiveness and abundance of land resources in the district. An Iowa land office, for example, often completed its work within a decade;

some of the Nevada land offices, on the other hand, did very little business over a very long period of time.

Most of the work on the maps from which our slides were made was done by Edwin Karn of the history department with technical assistance from Randall Sale of the cartographic laboratory of the University of Wisconsin. The results of their work were so impressive that the Dorsey Press arranged for them to collaborate in redrawing the maps for this atlas. Their work for this atlas sets a high standard of excellence.

These maps tell the attentive student much about the expansion of the Republic. They suggest much more. The new land occupied during each successive decade was taken up by people who had moved from the older American communities or from Europe. The Swedish novelist Wilhelm Moberg in one of his stories tells about a Swedish boy who grew up under the impression that a relative was somebody from the family who had emigrated to America. The area shown as newly settled during each successive decade represents land occupied by somebody's relatives. There is another aspect of the story suggested by the constantly advancing lines of settlement. The American Indians claimed but could not hold these lands against the relentless push of the whites. Thus the advance of the whites meant the retreat and disruption, sometimes the total destruction, of the Indian tribes. These people could know the bitter import of Emily Dickinson's statement that it is the vanquished, not the victors, who know the full melancholy meaning of victory.

VERNON CARSTENSEN
University of Wisconsin

INTRODUCTION

FROM the seventeenth century to the end of the nineteenth, much of American history has been the dynamic story of expansion and land occupation. English colonists moved inland slowly for a century and a half before planting their first tiny settlements beyond the Appalachians. By the end of the eighteenth century the tempo had increased. Expansion of settlement moved so rapidly that, in 1890, only one hundred years after the first official United States census, the Census Bureau declared that it could no longer draw a frontier line dividing settled from unsettled lands. Indeed, Frederick Jackson Turner, the noted historian of the American West, found the key to American history and to the American character in this westward movement of people. Despite its importance, the speed and direction of expansion is not easy to follow on existing maps. This series of maps is designed to illustrate that process of land acquisition, exploration, and occupation from nationhood to the twentieth century. Specifically the series illustrates: (1) national territorial growth; (2) organization of territories and states; (3) spread of settlement across the continent; (4) establishment and closing of federal land offices disposing of public lands; and (5) primary explorations and routes probing beyond the frontier of settlement. A map for each decade from 1790 through 1900 makes it possible to present this data sequentially and adjacent maps facilitate ready comparison. The accompanying text offers a summary of some of the data presented graphically by each map.

Population data follow the *Statistical Atlas of the United States,* prepared for the census of 1900, except for west coast population in 1850 and 1860, which is illustrated only in the 1870 *Statistical Atlas.* Population distribution appears as in the *Statistical Atlases* but it has been plotted on a more accurate continental map. Since our interest was in areas settled or being settled, we employed only three density categories: less than two people per square mile; two to six per square mile, the census definition

of a frontier area; and six or more per square mile, defined by the census as settled area. For 1850 and 1860 we supplied approximate distribution data based on census returns to avoid the misleading impression that would result from omission in the area between the one hundredth meridian and west coast settlements. Because we were concerned with expansion in the United States, we have not shown population data for areas not yet claimed by the United States, even though that population may have been extensive and have had densities greater than six per square mile. Boundaries shown are those pertaining in the census year for that decade. If several changes occurred within ten years, we have illustrated only the last boundary for the decade. Small boundary adjustments and disputes between states were omitted. Areas in dispute between the United States and other nations are indicated between the extreme claims of the two nations. Names of states and dates of admission are included only on the map that marks the end of the decade during which statehood was conferred. Territories are named as long as territorial status pertains, but the date of their establishment appears only once. Land offices are shown as listed in government publications of the census year. When several changes occur within a decade, they are not included. The explorations and routes were chosen to show major probes into unknown or little known areas or to illustrate important routes into unoccupied lands. After the railroad explorations of the 1850's, no further explorations are shown since by that date the continent held few important unknown areas. Beginning with 1860 we have plotted the development of some major railroad links across the American West.

We have, we hope, succeeded in illustrating the speed and direction of the settlement of the United States together with the explorations and agencies which made possible the spread of population across so vast an area in so short a time.

1790

In 1790 the territorial boundaries of the United States were those established by the Treaty of Paris in 1783 ending the American Revolution. Great Britain's Canadian colonies and the Great Lakes bounded the new nation on the north; the Mississippi River and Spanish Florida formed the western and southern boundaries. Two areas remained in dispute. The United States and Great Britain did not agree on the northern boundary of Maine and, in the West, Spain contested the southern boundary. The Union consisted of the original thirteen states, with Maine a district of Massachusetts and Vermont part of New York. Virginia and Georgia still extended west to the Mississippi River. Two territories comprised the rest of the national domain. The Ordinance of 1787, passed by Congress and adopted by the new Constitutional government in 1789, established a political framework for the Northwest Territory. This area included present-day Ohio, Indiana, Illinois, Michigan, Wisconsin, and a part of Minnesota. The Southwest Territory, established in 1790, gave political organization to what became Tennessee.

In 1790 President Washington authorized the first decennial census and the difficult job of conducting a systematic headcount began. When completed the count revealed a United States population of over 3,900,000, excluding the Northwest Territory where no enumeration was made. Most settlement lay between the Atlantic seaboard and the Appalachian mountain chain, extending continuously from Maine to southern Georgia. Sparse population inhabited the Maine coast, eastern New Jersey, and the Carolina and Georgia coasts. Except for these areas, the coastal region was well populated. Fingers of settlement extended beyond the main body of population into New Hampshire and to Lake Champlain in the North, and along the rich Mohawk River valley into western New York. Substantial settlement existed near Pittsburgh on the upper Ohio River in western Pennsylvania. Other settlements stretched into the Southwest Territory along the upper Tennessee River. Several isolated bodies of settlement had sprung up beyond the mountain barrier as well. The largest of these was south of the Ohio River in the lush lands of Kentucky. Smaller bodies of settlement grew up in the valleys of the Kanawha River in western Virginia, on the Cumberland River in the Southwest Territory around Nashville, and at the Marietta settlement on the Ohio River. Settlements related to the fur trade existed at Detroit on Lake Erie, at Mackinac and Sault Sainte Marie on the upper peninsula of Michigan, at Green Bay and Prairie du Chien in the Wisconsin area, at Cahokia and Kaskaskia on the Mississippi, and at Vincennes on the Wabash River. Other islands of settlement appeared in far western Virginia near the Mississippi-Ohio River junction, in southern New York, on Lake Ontario, and in western Pennsylvania.

In 1785 Congress adopted a land ordinance which prescribed a system of orderly rectangular surveys and auction sales for the federal lands in the Northwest Territory. By 1787 the government had surveyed a small area west of Pennsylvania and offered it for sale at auction in New York. Sales were few.

Many settlers moving west in this period followed rivers and streams, but many others crossed the Appalachian barrier by three overland routes. Braddock's Road, built by British troops under General Edward Braddock in 1755, traversed Maryland and swung north to Fort Pitt at the forks of the Ohio River. Forbes' Road, cut by troops under General John Forbes in 1758, gave access to the forks of the Ohio from eastern Pennsylvania. The Wilderness Road, blazed by Daniel Boone for Judge Richard Henderson in 1775, established a route through Cumberland Gap to the Kentucky settlements at Boonesborough and Harrodsburg. Connecting with the Great Valley Road in Virginia, it provided a continuous route from the Potomac River, along the Shenandoah Valley, across the mountains and into Kentucky.

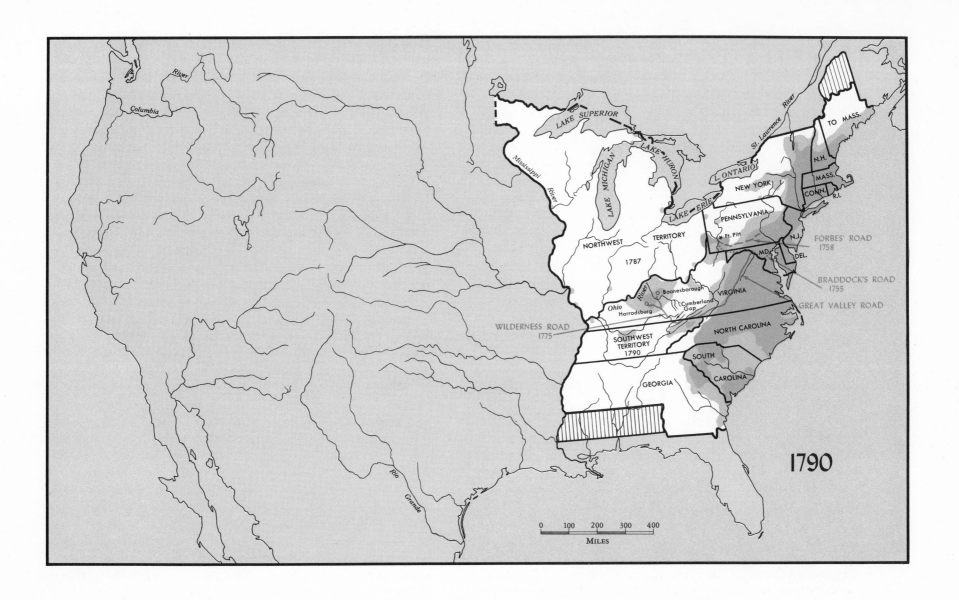

Columbia *River*

Mississippi *River*

LAKE SUPERIOR

LAKE MICHIGAN

LAKE HURON

LAKE ERIE

L. ONTARIO

St. Lawrence *River*

NORTHWEST TERRITORY
1787

N.H.

MASS.

TO MASS.

NEW YORK

CONN.

R.I.

PENNSYLVANIA

Ft. Pitt

N.J.

MD.

DEL.

FORBES' ROAD
1758

BRADDOCK'S ROAD
1755

GREAT VALLEY ROAD

Ohio *River*

Boonesborough

Harrodsburg

Cumberland Gap

VIRGINIA

WILDERNESS ROAD
1775

SOUTHWEST TERRITORY
1790

NORTH CAROLINA

SOUTH CAROLINA

GEORGIA

Rio Grande

1790

0   100   200   300   400

MILES

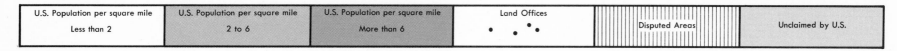

| U.S. Population per square mile | U.S. Population per square mile | U.S. Population per square mile | Land Offices | | Disputed Areas | Unclaimed by U.S. |
| Less than 2 | 2 to 6 | More than 6 | | | | |

1800

The international boundaries of the United States changed little between 1790 and 1800. Although the nation did not acquire new territory, in 1795 the Treaty of San Lorenzo, or Pinckney's Treaty, with Spain settled the disputed southwest border at the line claimed by the United States. Population growth and spreading settlement brought several internal boundary changes. In 1791 Vermont became the fourteenth state, reducing New York to its present size. Kentucky followed Vermont into the Union in 1792. In 1796 the Southwest Territory entered the Union as Tennessee. Georgia still extended west to the Mississippi River, but in 1798 Congress established Mississippi Territory to govern the old Spanish claim area. Congress created Indiana Territory in 1800 from the western half of the Northwest Territory.

The second United States census in 1800 revealed rapid population growth. Total population exceeded 5,300,000, an increase of more than 30 per cent in ten years. The distribution of population expanded the pattern of 1790. Settlement had pushed a little farther north in New Hampshire and Vermont. In New York the wedge of settlement in the Mohawk Valley broadened to extend from the Pennsylvania border to Lake Ontario. A narrow fringe of settlement continued along that shore and down the St. Lawrence Valley to connect with denser settlements around Lake Champlain. This formed a continuous ring of settlement encircling the vacant Adirondack mountain region in northern New York. In western Pennsylvania spreading population pushed a salient all the way north to Lake Erie. The Appalachian barrier continued to limit expansion in western Virginia and the Carolinas, but settlers in Georgia extended the frontier of settlement south and west to the border of Spanish Florida. In this main body of settlement many areas only sparsely settled in 1790 showed substantially heavier population. Population also ex-panded in areas beyond the mountains. In Kentucky population spread over much of the state and pushed across the Ohio River into the Northwest and Indiana Territories. Extending southward, settlement met and joined growing Tennessee settlements. A new island of settlement appeared in the Cleveland area on Lake Erie. In Mississippi Territory settlement stretched along the Mississippi River while a body of population sprang up in the interior along streams draining to the Gulf of Mexico.

The Harrison Land Law in 1800 established four new land offices for the sale of western lands located near the frontier of settlement in the Northwest Territory. This initiated the federal policy of providing land offices conveniently near the lands to be sold.

Zane's Trace, laid out across Ohio in 1796 by Ebenezer Zane, ran from Wheeling on the upper Ohio River through settlements at Zanesville and Chillicothe to the Ohio River opposite Limestone, Kentucky. It provided the first overland route across that area. The Natchez Trace, following an old Indian trail, became a well-traveled route connecting Nashville, Tennessee with Natchez on the lower Mississippi River.

Even then, while white settlement of the continent was still so closely tied to the Atlantic coast, explorers began investigating the western edge of the continent. In 1792 Captain George Vancouver, on an official exploring expedition for the British government, sailed up the Pacific coast from San Diego north to Alaska. In the course of his explorations he circumnavigated Vancouver Island, which bears his name, and located the mouth of the Columbia River. Earlier in the same year an American, Robert Gray, captain of the merchant ship *Columbia,* succeeded in crossing the treacherous bar at the mouth of that river he named for his ship. These two explorations formed part of the basis for conflicting United States and British claims to this area.

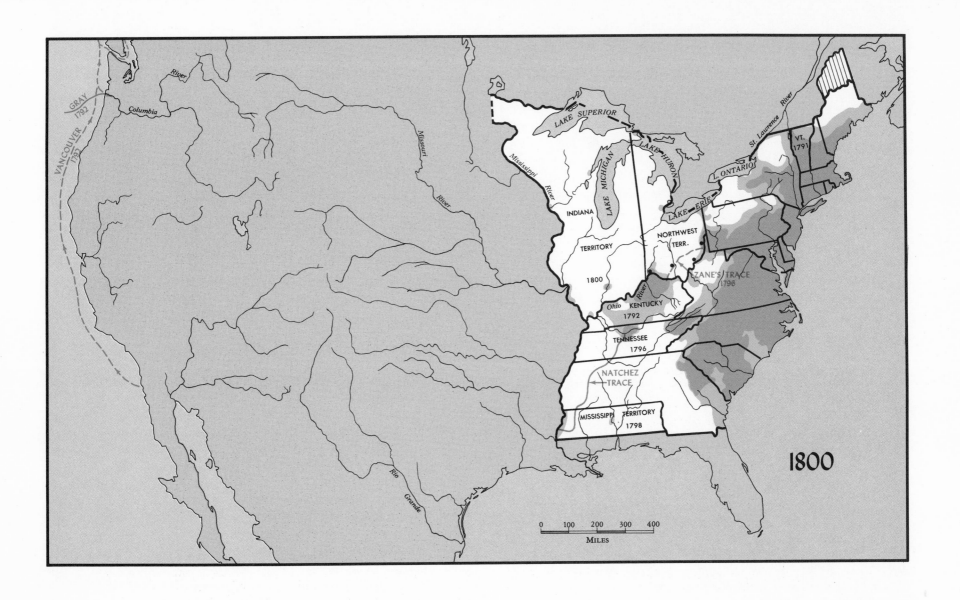

GRAY
1792

VANCOUVER
1792

Columbia River

Missouri River

LAKE SUPERIOR

Mississippi River

LAKE MICHIGAN

LAKE HURON

INDIANA

LAKE ERIE

NORTHWEST
TERR.

TERRITORY

1800

St. Lawrence River

L. ONTARIO

VT.
1791

ZANE'S TRACE
1796

Ohio River

KENTUCKY
1792

TENNESSEE
1796

NATCHEZ
TRACE

MISSISSIPPI TERRITORY
1798

Rio Grande

1800

0   100   200   300   400
MILES

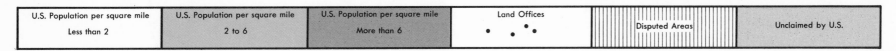

U.S. Population per square mile Less than 2	U.S. Population per square mile 2 to 6	U.S. Population per square mile More than 6	Land Offices	Disputed Areas	Unclaimed by U.S.

1810

In 1803 the vast Louisiana Purchase added nearly a million square miles to the national domain and gave the United States complete control of the Mississippi River. The limits of this purchase were indefinite and the map shows an approximate physical boundary based on Mississippi and Missouri River drainage basins. Spain still held Florida in 1803 and, because the boundaries of the purchase were not clear, part of west Florida came into dispute between the United States and Spain.

To provide political organization for these new lands, Congress in 1804 established Orleans Territory in the southern part of the purchase and in 1805 made the rest Louisiana Territory. Georgia ceded her western lands to the national government in 1802, and Congress added this area to Mississippi Territory. With Ohio statehood in 1803, Congress redivided the old Northwest Territory, creating Michigan Territory in 1805 and Illinois Territory in 1809.

The third decennial census enumerated over 7,200,000 people in 1810. The increase of over two million since 1800 was a gain of more than 30 per cent. Although vacant areas remained in the Adirondacks and along the Appalachian highlands, the westward spreading population made settlement continuous from the coast to Lake Erie and to western Kentucky and Tennessee. The lush lands open for settlement south of the Ohio attracted many more settlers than the partially surveyed lands to the north where periodic Indian raids made settlement hazardous. Indian holdings in Georgia delayed expansion in that state, but the southwestward trend of new land settlement is clear. The annexation of new territory brought into the United States substantial settlements around the mouth of the Mississippi and in nearby river valleys, reinforcing this trend. The St. Louis settlements, expanding southward along the Mississippi, also became American with the purchase. As population spread and land surveys progressed, Congress opened seven more land offices. In 1810 eleven offices sold federal lands in Mississippi and Indiana Territories as well as in Ohio.

In 1803 President Jefferson sent an expedition to explore the Missouri River and the "portages to the Pacific." Meriwether Lewis and William Clark led this expedition from St. Louis up the Missouri, across the continental divide, then down the Snake and Columbia Rivers to the Pacific. On their return in 1806 they split into two groups after crossing the mountains. Clark's contingent traveled down the Yellowstone to the Missouri, while Lewis's party explored north along the Marias River. After skirmishing with hostile Indians, Lewis returned to the Missouri and rejoined Clark at the mouth of the Yellowstone for the return trip down river. Meanwhile agents of the Northwest Fur Company explored west of the Rocky Mountains in Canada. Between 1807 and 1811 David Thompson, one of these agents, established trading posts throughout the Columbia River area and explored and mapped much of the territory from the Columbia north almost to Alaska.

Other less dramatic explorations were under way at the same time. In 1804 William Dunbar and George Hunter, sent by Jefferson to explore the Red River, traveled a short distance up the Red but then turned north along the Black and Ouachita Rivers to the Hot Springs area. Two years later Thomas Freeman, with Dunbar, led a second expedition up the Red which reached the present western border of Arkansas before Spanish troops halted their explorations. In 1806 Zebulon Pike led another government expedition into the new purchase to explore the Arkansas and Red Rivers. From St. Louis Pike led his party west, swung north to the Republican River, and then west along the Arkansas to the Pike's Peak region. When Pike's group headed south to the upper Rio Grande, Spanish troops captured them and conducted the party into Mexico.

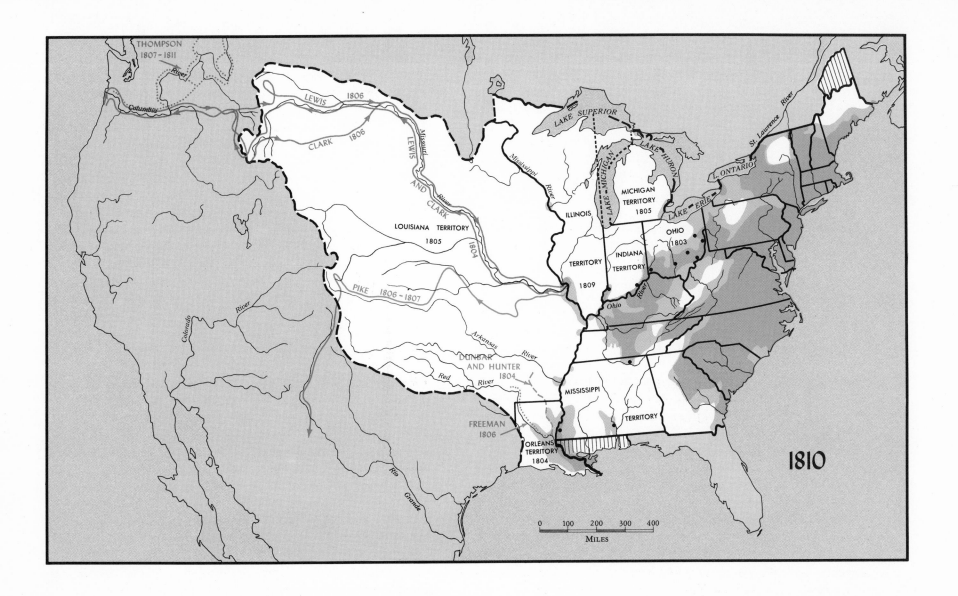

THOMPSON
1807-1811

Columbia River

LEWIS 1806

CLARK 1806

LEWIS AND CLARK

Missouri River

1804

LAKE SUPERIOR

Mississippi River

LAKE MICHIGAN

LAKE HURON

L. ONTARIO

St. Lawrence River

LAKE ERIE

MICHIGAN
TERRITORY
1805

ILLINOIS

LOUISIANA TERRITORY
1805

TERRITORY
1809

INDIANA
TERRITORY

OHIO
1803

PIKE 1806-1807

Colorado River

Arkansas River

DUNBAR
AND HUNTER
1804

Red River

Ohio River

FREEMAN
1806

MISSISSIPPI

ORLEANS
TERRITORY
1804

TERRITORY

Rio Grande

1810

0   100   200   300   400
MILES

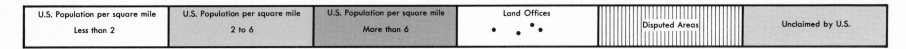

U.S. Population per square mile Less than 2	U.S. Population per square mile 2 to 6	U.S. Population per square mile More than 6	Land Offices	Disputed Areas	Unclaimed by U.S.

1820

Negotiations following the War of 1812 wrought major changes in America's boundaries. In 1818 the United States and Britain decided on the 49th parallel from the Lake of the Woods to the Rocky Mountains as the northern boundary of the Louisiana Purchase. The two nations agreed to open the Oregon country west of the Rockies for joint occupation until conflicting claims could be resolved.* American incursions into feebly held Spanish Florida led to its cession to the United States by Spain in the 1819 Adams-Onis Treaty. This treaty also fixed the southern boundary of the Louisiana Purchase.

Several new states and territories brought extensive internal boundary changes as well. In 1812 Orleans Territory became the state of Louisiana and Congress renamed the remainder of the Louisiana Purchase, Missouri Territory. In 1819 Congress created Arkansas Territory to govern the southern portion of that area. In 1817 Mississippi became a state and Alabama, a territory. Two years later, in 1819, Alabama also achieved statehood. In the Old Northwest, statehood for Indiana in 1816 and Illinois, 1818, enlarged the jurisdiction of Michigan Territory. In 1820 Maine separated from Massachusetts and became a state.

The census in 1820 showed that over 9,600,000 people lived in the United States. This again was more than a 30 per cent increase in population in ten years. The rapidly expanding population filled in much of the Appalachian highland unsettled in 1810, but small areas still remained vacant. With the easing of Indian hostilities and the extension of surveys, population spread rapidly into the old Northwest. The expanding Detroit settlements joined the burgeoning Ohio population along Lake Erie. Growing settlements pushed north of the Ohio River into Indiana and Illinois and connected with the rapidly developing settlements stretching up the Missouri and Mississippi Valleys around St. Louis. Tennessee settlement thrust south and west through Alabama and Mississippi to join enlarging Louisiana settlements. Indian land holdings still limited expansion in Georgia, Alabama, and Mississippi, but the southwesterly advance of population apparent in 1810 continued in this decade. Land offices for the sale of the public domain multiplied threefold from eleven in 1810 to thirty-four in 1820, and land offices operated in nine states and territories.

Before the outbreak of the War of 1812, John J. Astor sent an overland expedition to the mouth of the Columbia to meet a second seaborn group and establish a trading post for his Pacific Fur Company. In 1811 Wilson P. Hunt led these Astorians from St. Louis up the Missouri until hostile Indians forced him to strike west across the plains south of the Lewis and Clark route. After crossing the mountains he pushed down the Snake and Columbia Rivers and founded the post, Astoria. In 1812 Robert Stuart led a return expedition back along the Columbia and Snake but, swinging farther south than Hunt had, he crossed the continental divide near South Pass and then followed the Sweetwater and North Platte Rivers to the Missouri. His route along these rivers became the major immigrant trail west in later years. In 1819 Stephen H. Long led an army exploration up the Missouri River to Council Bluffs, where they spent the winter. Early in 1820 he headed west along the South Platte River to the Rocky Mountains near Long's Peak, then swung south along the face of the Rockies to the Canadian River. Long followed the Canadian to its junction, not with the expected Red River, but rather with the Arkansas River. He then continued along the Arkansas River to Fort Smith in western Arkansas where he ended his explorations.

*All of the Oregon country was open to joint occupation but Britain never claimed exclusive ownership. In 1818 she proposed the 45th parallel as the southern limit of joint occupation, shown here as the southern edge of disputed area.

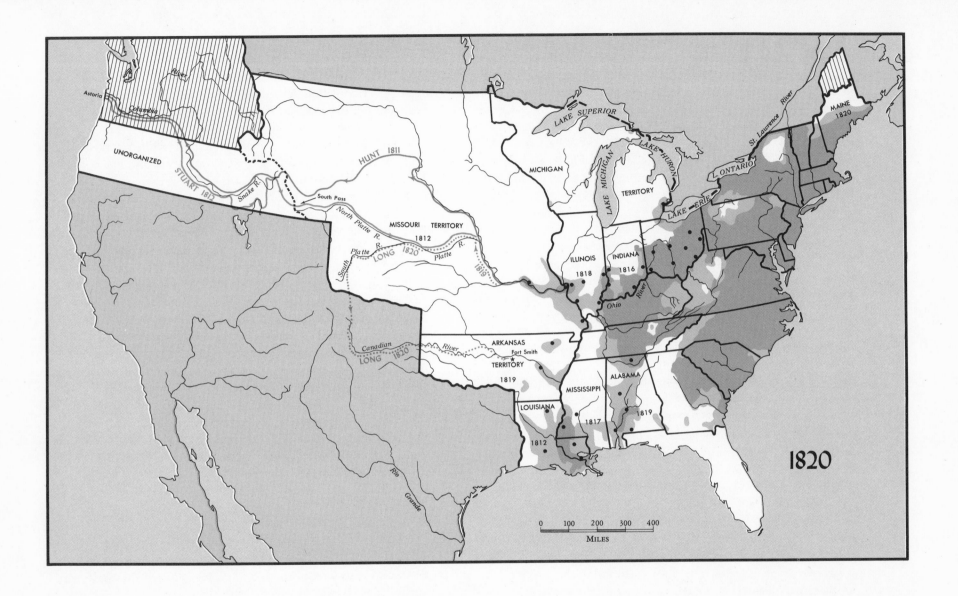

1820

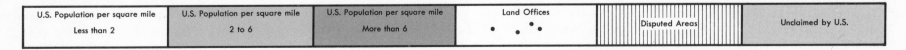

1830

In 1830 the British-American agreement for joint occupation of the Oregon country governed the unsettled northwestern boundary of the United States. The two powers also disputed the northeastern boundary, despite Maine's statehood. The "Missouri Compromise" seeking to resolve the growing controversy over expansion of Negro slavery, in 1821 allowed Missouri, a slave state, to enter the Union balancing Maine's admission as a free state the previous year. In 1822 Florida, acquired in 1819, joined Michigan and Arkansas in territorial status. The remaining area of the Louisiana Purchase and the Oregon country had no political organization after Missouri statehood.

The population of the United States passed 12,800,000 in 1830. For the fourth consecutive decade American population had grown more than 30 per cent. During this decade the distribution of settlement ended its earlier southwesterly trend and moved almost straight west. Coastal settlement pushed south into Florida Territory and farther north into Maine while the Appalachian highland continued to fill in. The beginnings of Indian relocation in the South allowed rapid expansion in Georgia and the Gulf states, and a nearly solid body of settlement now extended from the Atlantic coast to the salients thrusting up the valleys of the Missouri and Arkansas Rivers. Isolated settlements sprang up in western Michigan and in the lead mining region of northern Illinois. The pressure of settlement brought another increase in federal land offices from thirty-four to forty-two in 1830, and every state and territory with public lands to sell had at least two land offices in operation.

Beyond the area of American settlement, trade and exploration continued unabated. Stephen H. Long, sent in 1823 to explore the Minnesota River and the northern United States boundary between the Red River of the North and Lake Superior, led his party from Prairie du Chien up the Mississippi and Minnesota Rivers. He portaged to the Red and followed it to Lake Winnipeg. Long then explored southeast to Lake of the Woods and Lake Superior. In 1824-25 Peter S. Ogden, a Hudson's Bay Company agent, headed east from Fort Vancouver on the Colum-

bia, and across the mountains to the three forks of the Missouri River. Hostile Indians turned him back westward to the Salmon River. He then cut south to the Snake River, followed it to the Bear River, and thus to the Great Salt Lake. Although he probably was not the original discoverer of Salt Lake, Ogden's is one of the first documented accounts.

The old trail to Santa Fe became an established trade route when Mexico adopted less stringent trade controls. From western Missouri it crossed to the Arkansas River and continued west along that stream. The "Mountain Division" ran north of the river to Bent's Fort, then turned south through difficult Raton Pass to Santa Fe. The more direct "Cimarron Division" crossed the river and proceeded directly to Santa Fe across the plains. This shorter and less rugged route substituted the hazards of water shortage for those of rough terrain. From Santa Fe Americans traded west to California. The "Gila Trail" followed the 1827-29 route of traders James O. Pattie and his father, Sylvester. Following the Rio Grande south from Santa Fe they cut west along the Salt and Gila Rivers, crossed the Colorado, and continued west to San Diego. In 1830 William Wolfskill, another trader, established the "Old Spanish Trail" which turned northwest from Santa Fe into present-day Utah, crossed the upper Colorado, and then swung southwest along the Sevier and Virgin Rivers, through Cajon Pass to the Los Angeles area. The most important explorations in this area were made from 1826 to 1829 by Jedediah Smith, an American "mountain man." He left Salt Lake in 1826 and headed southwest along the Sevier and Virgin Rivers and into California through Cajon Pass, swung north into the San Joaquin River Valley, and returned to Salt Lake across the desert. In 1827 he took the same route to California, and after a stop at Monterey, continued north up the Sacramento River and then west to the coast. As he followed the coast northward, his party was attacked by Indians, but Smith was able to continue north to the Columbia River and, late in 1828, reached Fort Vancouver. In 1829 he explored up the Columbia, down the Bitterroot River, and through Lemhi Pass to the trappers' rendezvous at Pierre's Hole.

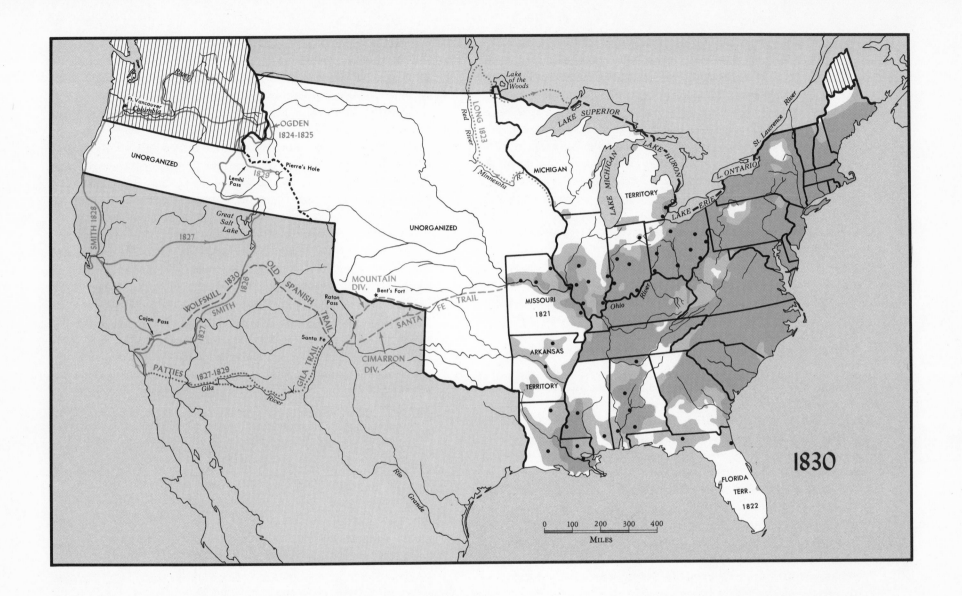

1830

U.S. Population per square mile
Less than 2

U.S. Population per square mile
2 to 6

U.S. Population per square mile
More than 6

Land Offices

Disputed Areas

Unclaimed by U.S.

1840

The limits of the United States were the same in 1840 as they had been ten years before, with the northeastern and northwestern boundaries still indefinite. On the southwestern border, however, a new element emerged — the independent Republic of Texas. Formerly a state of Mexico settled largely by Americans, Texas won her independence in 1836 and the following year requested annexation by the United States. Because of the problems annexation posed in the growing sectional controversy and in American relations with Mexico, Congress denied the petition. In 1836 Arkansas, and in 1837, Michigan entered the Union, preserving the sectional balance between northern and southern states. When Congress reduced Michigan's boundaries in 1836, Wisconsin became a territory. Florida's territorial status continued unchanged. In 1838 Congress erected Iowa Territory across the Mississippi River in the Louisiana Purchase area, but the remainder of the Purchase and the Oregon country lacked political organization.

The 1840 census demonstrated that the population had grown more than four million in ten years, to reach a total of over seventeen million, a 30 per cent increase for the fifth consecutive decade. The southwesterly trend of new land settlement, which had ended by 1830, was reversed in 1840. Population attracted by lead mining, lumbering, and fertile farm lands moved rapidly northward. Settlement moved only a little farther west, but settlers filled in the area around earlier western salients. The removal of eastern Indian tribes to lands west of the Mississippi River prevented legal expansion beyond the western boundaries of Arkansas and Missouri. Some gaps still remained in the settlement of those states. Settlers continued to spread across the Gulf states and population pushed farther into Florida. Despite this expansion in the South, however, the most striking movement of population in this decade was toward the North. The Maine frontier moved northward and rapid settlement stretched north through Indiana and Illinois, well into Michigan, and northwest into Wisconsin and Iowa Territories. To sell public lands in these areas of rapid growth Congress had increased the number of land offices from forty-two to sixty-six by 1840.

In 1832 Major Benjamin L. E. Bonneville, on leave from the army, led an expedition west to investigate possibilities in the fur trade. In 1833 he sent "mountain man" James Walker to explore in the basin and range country. Leaving Bonneville's camp, Walker proceeded to Salt Lake and then struck out across the desert to the west. He hit the Humboldt River and followed it until it disappeared in the Carson Sink. He then turned west, crossed the mountains into California, and continued to Monterey. From there Walker moved south through California, skirting the mountains and, turning east at Walker's Pass, crossed them. He headed north along the east face of the mountains until he again found the Humboldt and then retraced his route to Salt Lake. In 1834 Nathaniel Wyeth organized his second expedition to form a trading company in the Oregon country. He was accompanied by Reverend Jason Lee, a Methodist missionary who proposed to establish the first American mission in the Pacific Northwest. From Independence Wyeth's party traveled up the Missouri River and turned west along the Platte River. They paralleled Stuart's earlier route along the North Platte and Sweetwater Rivers and through South Pass. Once across the continental divide they cut north to the Snake River and proceeded along the Snake to the Columbia. They then followed the Columbia to Fort Vancouver and the valley of the Willamette River. The routes of Walker and Wyeth taken together comprise the two great immigrant routes west in later years. Wyeth's route through South Pass to Oregon became the Oregon Trail, while the Walker route, beginning near South Pass and following the Humboldt River southwest across the basin and range country, became the main route to California.

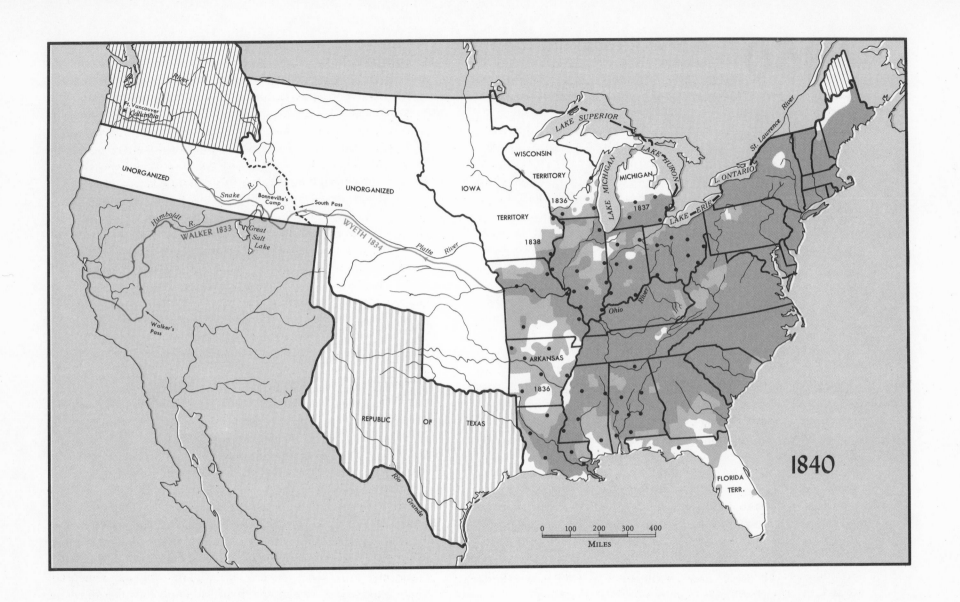

UNORGANIZED

Fr. Vancouver
Columbia
River
Snake R.
Humboldt R.
WALKER 1833
Great Salt Lake
Bonneville's Camp
South Pass
WYETH 1834
Platte River
Walker's Pass

UNORGANIZED

WISCONSIN
TERRITORY
1836

IOWA
TERRITORY
1838

MICHIGAN
1837

LAKE SUPERIOR
LAKE MICHIGAN
LAKE HURON
LAKE ERIE
L. ONTARIO
St. Lawrence River

ARKANSAS
1836

Ohio River

REPUBLIC   OF   TEXAS

Rio Grande

FLORIDA
TERR.

1840

0   100   200   300   400
MILES

U.S. Population per square mile Less than 2	U.S. Population per square mile 2 to 6	U.S. Population per square mile More than 6	Land Offices	Disputed Areas	Unclaimed by U.S.

1850

In this decade two agreements established the present northern boundary of the United States. In 1842 the Webster-Ashburton Treaty with Great Britain settled the long dispute over the Maine boundary and, despite American bluster about "Fifty-four Forty or Fight," negotiations in 1846 fixed the northwestern boundary at the 49th parallel. In 1845, after long debate, Congress annexed Texas, which led to war with Mexico in 1846. In 1848 Americans captured Mexico City. The Treaty of Guadalupe Hidalgo, which ended the Mexican war, established the boundary of Texas at the Rio Grande and provided for the cession to the United States of New Mexico and California. Florida joined Texas in statehood in 1845 and Congress balanced the admission of these two southern states by granting statehood to Iowa in 1846 and Wisconsin in 1848. Discovery of gold in California in 1848 brought it a rapid influx of people, and as part of the "Compromise of 1850" California became a state. With the acquisition of new lands and the erection of new states, Congress established new territories. In 1848 Oregon Territory and in 1849 Minnesota Territory emerged in the North. Congress created Utah and New Mexico Territories in 1850 to provide government for the acquisitions from Mexico. The remaining part of the Louisiana Purchase continued without political organization.

The census showed continuing growth of American population. The sixth consecutive ten-year increase of over 30 per cent brought United States population to more than 23,100,000 in 1850. Except for light population along the Gulf coast of Texas, a further push into Iowa, and isolated bodies of settlement in Minnesota river valleys and northern Wisconsin, the frontier of settlement changed little. On the west coast, however, settlements sprang up along Oregon's Willamette River Valley and around Puget Sound. With the gold rush, settlement grew rapidly near California ports and in interior river valleys. The Census Bureau provided no maps for the plains area, but by 1850 settlement was well established around Salt Lake and on the upper Rio Grande near Taos and Santa Fe. In 1850 no land offices had yet opened either on the west coast or in the plains and only one more opened in the older area, to bring the total to sixty-seven.

The Oregon and California Trails along routes established by Walker and Wyeth became well traveled in this decade. Exploration in the plains and mountains continued. Captain John C. Fremont led three official explorations in this decade. In 1842 he left Missouri and explored up the North Platte-Sweetwater River route through South Pass to Fremont's Peak, returning by way of the Platte to Council Bluffs. The following year he again explored up the South Platte, and made a swing south to Pueblo and back, before continuing north through South Pass. He followed the usual Snake-Columbia River route until he connected with the maritime exploration of Captain Charles Wilkes. With his official mission thus completed, Fremont headed south through Oregon toward California. He continued south along the east slope of the Sierra Nevada and despite extremely hazardous winter conditions, succeeded in crossing the mountains into California. Traveling south in California he crossed the mountains at Cajon Pass and swung north up the Spanish Trail to Lake Utah. Fremont then visited Bent's Fort and followed the Smoky Hill fork of the Kansas River back to the Missouri River in 1844. The next year he again headed west along this return route. From Bent's Fort he turned north to Salt Lake and along the Humboldt River route to California. He had traveled north from California to the Lake Klamath area when news of the Mexican war ended his journey.

In 1846 a migration across the plains began. The Latter Day Saints, driven by persecution from their Nauvoo, Illinois community, crossed southern Iowa and headed west along the Platte River. Their well-organized expedition stayed north of the North Platte and Sweetwater Rivers rather than following the usual south bank. After crossing the divide at South Pass the Mormons moved southwest to Salt Lake where in 1847 they established their new community.

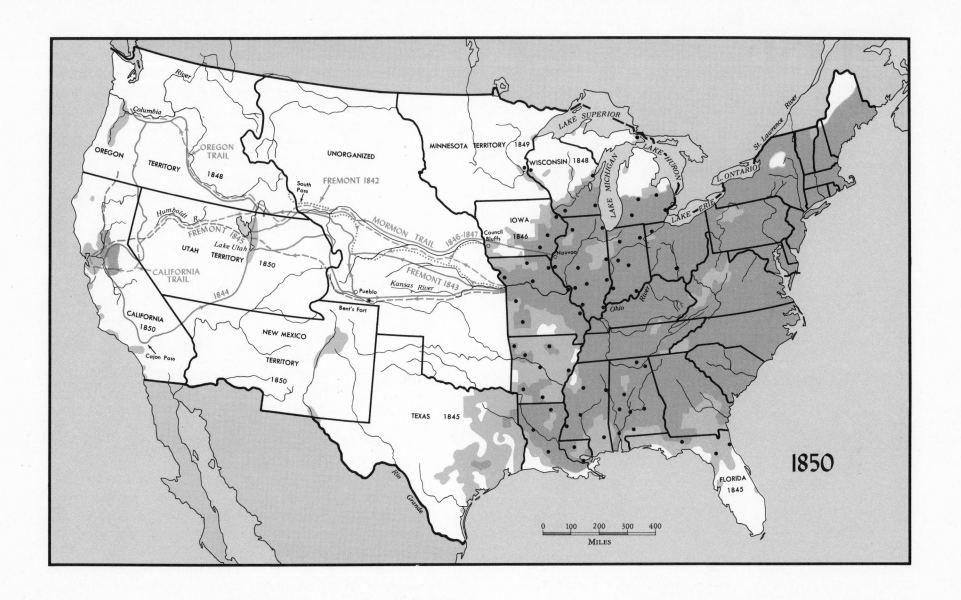

OREGON
TERRITORY
1848

Columbia River

OREGON TRAIL

South Pass

Humboldt R.

FREMONT 1845

UTAH
TERRITORY
1850

Lake Utah

CALIFORNIA
TRAIL

1844

CALIFORNIA
1850

Cajon Pass

FREMONT 1842

MORMON TRAIL 1846-1847

Council Bluffs

Nauvoo

FREMONT 1843

Kansas River

Pueblo

Bent's Fort

NEW MEXICO
TERRITORY
1850

TEXAS   1845

Rio Grande

UNORGANIZED

MINNESOTA TERRITORY 1849

WISCONSIN 1848

IOWA
1846

LAKE SUPERIOR

LAKE MICHIGAN

LAKE HURON

LAKE ERIE

Ohio River

L. ONTARIO

St. Lawrence River

FLORIDA
1845

1850

0   100   200   300   400
MILES

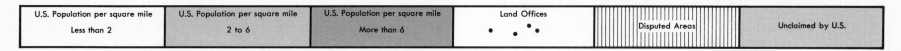

1860

In the 1850's rising interest in a railroad to the Pacific along a southern route made the Gila River Valley important. In 1853, to insure that the route would lie in American territory, Congress obtained from Mexico the Gadsden Purchase, a small area south of the Gila River. This tract gave the United States its present southwest boundary.

New Mexico and Utah continued as territories, while Washington Territory, erected in 1853, provided political organization for settlements north of the Columbia River and around Puget Sound. In 1854 the conflict over slavery expansion flared up anew when Kansas and Nebraska became territories. Minnesota, in 1858, and Oregon, in 1859, entered the Union destroying the precarious balance between slave and free states and adding further to the drift toward civil war. A narrow area between the Missouri River and Minnesota's western border, and Indian lands in the Oklahoma area, still lacked government.

Between 1850 and 1860 American population continued to grow more than 30 per cent per decade. The 1860 census revealed a population of over 31,400,000. This fast-growing population continued to push northward in Michigan and Wisconsin, while scattered settlements grew up along the shores of Lake Superior and in Minnesota's Red River Valley. Expanding settlements in Minnesota merged with populated areas in Wisconsin and Iowa. Settlers spreading across Iowa thrust fingers of settlement into Kansas and Nebraska Territories. Population in Texas consolidated and began moving west and north. West coast settlements in California, Oregon, and Washington Territory also grew in size and density. The Census Bureau failed to map population in the western plains and mountains, but the communities on the upper Rio Grande and around Salt Lake continued to expand, and new settlements sprang up along the eastern Rockies. The number of land offices grew from sixty-seven to seventy-eight and were concentrated heavily in the West, where settlement was most rapid.

In the early 1850's agitation for a transcontinental railroad to connect the west coast with the Mississippi Valley increased greatly. Competition between midwestern cities to become its eastern terminus contributed to the strain between North and South. The federal government entered the controversy in 1854-55 by sponsoring expeditions to determine the suitability of proposed routes for railroad building. Isaac I. Stevens, governor of Washington Territory, commanded the most northerly exploration. He explored north and west from St. Paul on the Mississippi and along the Missouri River, while Captain George McClennan probed the Cascade Mountains for railroad passes. Together they explored several routes through the mountains to western terminals on the Columbia and Puget Sound. Widespread dissatisfaction with Stevens' report led the Washington Territorial Assembly to authorize Frederick W. Landers, a civil engineer with Stevens' party, to investigate the feasibility of railroad construction along the Oregon Trail from Missouri through South Pass to Puget Sound. A more central route explored by Lieutenant John W. Gunnison lay between the 38th and 39th parallels. After exploring passes through the Colorado Rockies, Gunnison headed west across Utah where hostile Indians killed him and several members of his party. Lieutenant Edward G. Beckwith, another officer with the expedition, took command and led the party north to Salt Lake. He first investigated a 41st parallel route east through the mountains, then turned west across the interior basin and located two suitable passes through the mountains to California. Still another party under Lieutenant Amiel W. Whipple examined a route along the 35th parallel. Heading west from Fort Smith, Whipple's party explored along the Canadian River, to the upper Rio Grande, and then through difficult country to the Colorado River. They crossed into California at the "Needles" and pushed west to Los Angeles. Farther south Lieutenant John G. Parke explored a route east along the Gila River from California to El Paso on the Rio Grande, while Captain John Pope led a party from El Paso east through Texas to Fort Washita in present-day Oklahoma. On the west coast Lieutenant Robert S. Williamson, assisted by Lieutenant Henry L. Abbott, investigated mountain passes in southern California and explored possible routes for a railroad connecting California and Oregon. This series of government-financed explorations produced valuable data on the resources of western America, but provided no solution to the railroad problem.

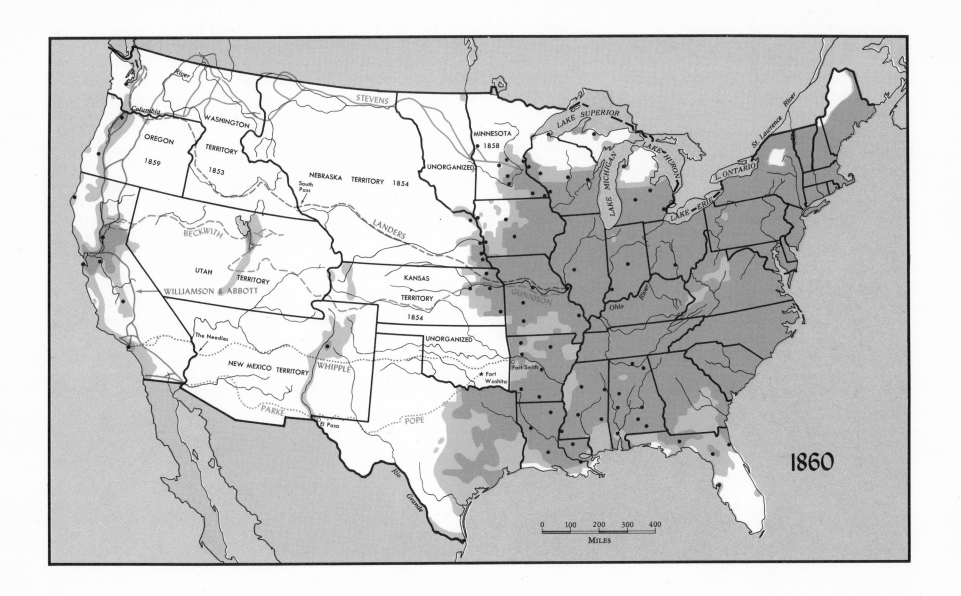

OREGON 1859

WASHINGTON TERRITORY 1853

STEVENS

Columbia River

MINNESOTA 1858

NEBRASKA TERRITORY 1854

UNORGANIZED

South Pass

BECKWITH

LANDERS

UTAH TERRITORY

WILLIAMSON & ABBOTT

KANSAS TERRITORY 1854

GUNNISON

Ohio River

The Needles

NEW MEXICO TERRITORY

WHIPPLE

UNORGANIZED

Fort Smith

Fort Washita

PARKE

POPE

El Paso

Rio Grande

LAKE SUPERIOR

LAKE MICHIGAN

LAKE HURON

LAKE ERIE

L. ONTARIO

St. Lawrence River

1860

0   100   200   300   400

MILES

| U.S. Population per square mile Less than 2 | U.S. Population per square mile 2 to 6 | U.S. Population per square mile More than 6 | Land Offices | Disputed Areas | Unclaimed by U.S. |

1870

From 1861 to 1865, civil war overshadowed the persistent territorial expansion that had fanned the flame of conflict. Although war slowed westward expansion it did not halt it, and the West remained an important concern of government. By 1870, with the war ended, the march across the continent regained its full stride. Kansas and Nebraska entered the Union in 1861 and 1867 respectively. Circumstances of war led to the separation of Virginia's western counties and their admission to the Union in 1863 as the state of West Virginia. Nevada, given territorial status in 1861 at the beginning of the war, in 1864 became a state for reasons of wartime political expediency. The status of Washington, New Mexico, and Utah Territories remained unchanged during the war decade, but the West was drastically redivided. In 1861 Colorado and Dakota became territories, and in 1863 Congress created Arizona and Idaho Territories. Montana achieved territorial organization in 1864 to round out the wartime redivision. In 1868 Wyoming too became a territory, but the Oklahoma area composed of Indian holdings remained unorganized.

Because of wartime casualties and the deterrent effect of war on immigration, the rate of population growth in the United States for the first time fell below the 30 per cent decennial increase that had prevailed since 1790. By 1870, however, the population had grown substantially and increased by over 7,100,000 to reach a total of more than 38,500,000. Settlement spread northwest in Minnesota and pushed substantially west into the grasslands of Kansas and Nebraska. Texas settlement also expanded west and south, but Indian holdings in Oklahoma limited westward movement of settlement from Arkansas. In 1870, for the first time, the Census Bureau mapped population distribution across the entire continent, revealing a long tongue of settlement extending along the eastern fringe of the Rocky Mountains from Wyoming south through Colorado and New Mexico to the Rio Grande in Texas. The Utah settlements and coastal settlements in California, Oregon, and Washington continued to expand. In addition to these fairly large bodies of population, a great scattering of small isolated settlements sprang up in mining and agricultural areas from Idaho and Montana southward into Texas. Congress in 1862 passed the long-awaited Homestead Act, which allowed settlers to acquire 160 acres of the public domain simply by living on it and paying a small fee. By 1870 land offices responsible for administering this act had opened in every western state and territory. The locations of land offices, totaling eighty-five rather than seventy-eight as in 1860, illustrate the areas of greatest activity. Only nineteen of the offices remained east of the Mississippi River and, of these, eleven lay in the unsettled timber country of Wisconsin and Michigan.

In 1869 the Union Pacific and Central Pacific met to form the first transcontinental railroad. Congress in 1862 provided for two companies, financed largely by federal loans and land grants, to build a railroad over a central route. The Central Pacific was to build west to east and the Union Pacific from east to west. In 1863 the Central Pacific began laying track eastward but made slow progress crossing the Sierra Nevada Mountains. The Union Pacific building west from Omaha also progressed slowly until the war's end released labor and capital for construction. Since federal land grants depended on the number of miles of railroad built, each company raced the other across the continent in order to secure the greatest possible benefits for itself. As the two companies laid track across Utah from opposite directions, they reached a peak of speed which raised output to ten miles per day. In 1869 the two roads finally met at Promontory, Utah, near Ogden, where a golden spike formally joined them into a single transcontinental line. Ironically, despite the furor in the 1850's, the first transcontinental railroad followed none of the routes surveyed by the government in the previous decade.

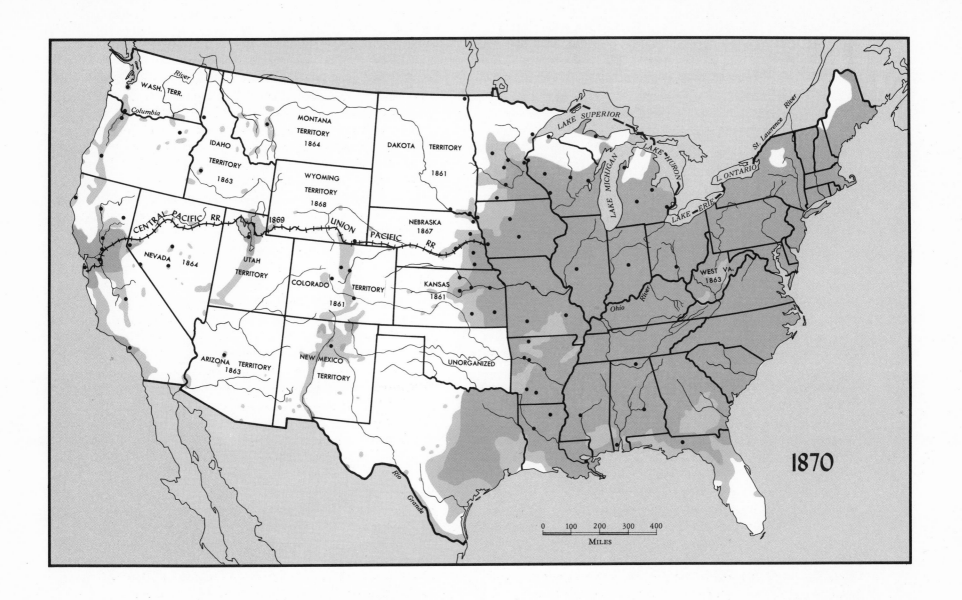

1870

WASH. TERR.

Columbia River

IDAHO TERRITORY 1863

MONTANA TERRITORY 1864

DAKOTA TERRITORY 1861

WYOMING TERRITORY 1868

NEVADA 1864

CENTRAL PACIFIC RR

1869

UNION PACIFIC RR

UTAH TERRITORY

COLORADO TERRITORY 1861

NEBRASKA 1867

KANSAS 1861

ARIZONA TERRITORY 1863

NEW MEXICO TERRITORY

UNORGANIZED

Rio Grande

LAKE SUPERIOR

LAKE MICHIGAN

LAKE HURON

LAKE ERIE

L. ONTARIO

St. Lawrence River

WEST VA. 1863

Ohio River

| 0 | 100 | 200 | 300 | 400 |

MILES

| U.S. Population per square mile | U.S. Population per square mile | U.S. Population per square mile | Land Offices | | Disputed Areas | Unclaimed by U.S. |
| Less than 2 | 2 to 6 | More than 6 | | | | |

1880

By 1880 the continental United States had settled down within the familiar boundaries. The political maturity of Canada and Mexico made any further territorial additions unlikely. Internally the reconstructed states of the Confederacy had reentered the Union without boundary changes, except for the state of West Virginia, severed from Virginia during the War. In 1876 Colorado Territory joined the ranks of statehood, while Washington, Idaho, Montana, Wyoming, Utah, Arizona, and New Mexico retained territorial status. These territories had assumed their final boundaries. Dakota Territory lacked only a division into northern and southern portions to achieve its final form. Indian lands without formal political organization still made up present-day Oklahoma, although they did reveal the shape of the future state. By 1880, then, except for the division of the Dakotas, the present pattern of state boundaries had emerged.

Between 1870 and 1880 natural increase and resurgent European immigration brought phenomenal population growth. The addition of more than 11,600,000 people to the American nation in ten years restored growth to the 30 per cent per decade increase of the pre-war period and brought the total population to over 50,100,000. Vacant areas in southern Florida, Maine, northern Michigan, and Wisconsin receded as new settlement pushed into these unoccupied lands. The primary frontier of settlement, however, continued to move westward. Settlers pressing beyond Minnesota into Dakota Territory rapidly filled in the valley of the Red River of the North to the Canadian border and beyond. In Nebraska and Kansas agricultural settlement expanding along river valleys reached almost to their western borders. Indian holdings still prevented settlement moving west from Arkansas, but rapid westward expansion in Kansas to the north and Texas to the south nearly surrounded these lands. The large body of settlement along the face of the Rockies grew in all directions. In Wyoming settlers pushed north and east, while in Colorado and New Mexico they extended both east and west to exploit the possibilities of mining and agriculture. Limited amounts of available arable land curtailed expansion in Utah, but population grew in density. Substantial bodies of settlement attracted by discoveries of mineral wealth sprang up in the Black Hills of western Dakota and along river valleys of Idaho and western Montana. In Arizona and Nevada fair-sized settlements developed along the Humboldt River and in other areas where water was available. California exhibited rapid growth northward along the Sacramento Valley and westward into Nevada, but Washington and Oregon provided the most striking population advances on the Pacific coast. Settlement spread east along the Columbia into Idaho and filled in much of northern Oregon, while the rapidly growing population of Washington filled in the area between the Columbia and Puget Sound to the north.

By 1880 the frontier of settlement had ceased to be a simple movement west across the continent occupying mile after mile of agricultural land. While a westward movement of people did continue, settlement was also moving east from the Pacific coast and several large bodies of settlement in the interior were expanding both east and west. Less than adequate rainfall for traditional agriculture, and rugged terrain, made the solid settlement patterns familiar in areas further east impossible in much of the West. Settlement had to be selective. Areas of mineral resources, or of sufficient water, attracted settlers, while less-favored areas remained vacant. Despite areas of settlement in advance of the westward movement of population, however, in 1880 it was still possible to draw a north-south "frontier line" from the Canadian border to the Rio Grande, dividing the settled part of the United States from unsettled areas. Land offices, which increased from eighty-five in 1870 to ninety-six in 1880, illustrate the areas of greatest settlement. Only fifteen offices remained east of the Mississippi, while one-half of all land offices appeared beyond the "frontier line" in the rapidly growing West.

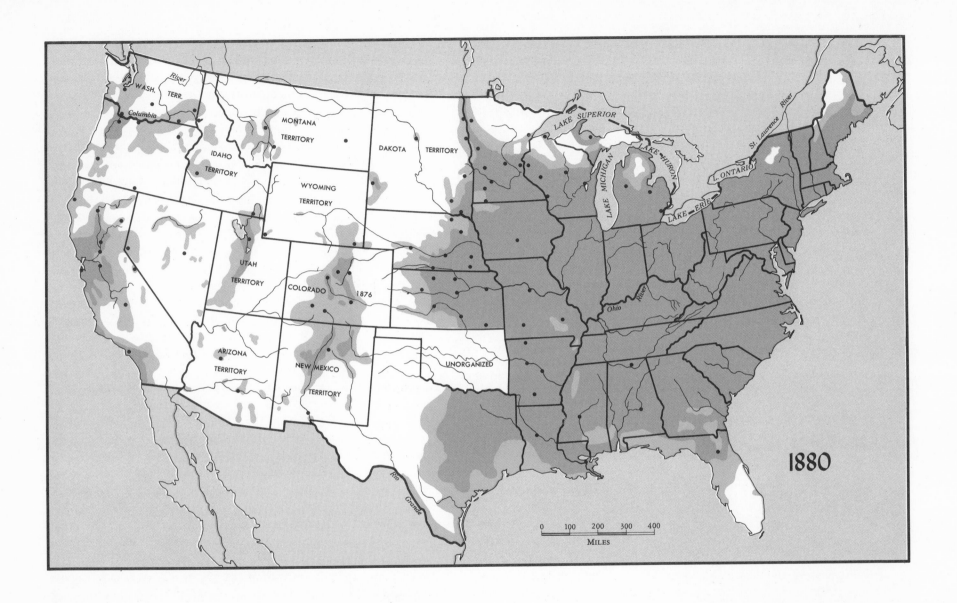

1880

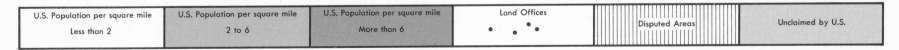

| U.S. Population per square mile Less than 2 | U.S. Population per square mile 2 to 6 | U.S. Population per square mile More than 6 | Land Offices | Disputed Areas | Unclaimed by U.S. |

1890

In the twenty-four years from the end of the Civil War until 1889 only two states entered the Union: Nebraska in 1867 and Colorado in 1876. For twelve years after Colorado's admission, political struggles between a Democratic Congress and a Republican President, or a Republican Congress and a Democratic President, prevented formation of new states. Finally, in 1888 election of Republican Benjamin Harrison to the presidency, and victory of Republicans in Congress, gave one-party control of both legislative and executive branches of government. The long delay over, in 1889 Washington and Montana, together with North and South Dakota made by splitting Dakota Territory in two, entered the union as the "Omnibus States." The admission of four new states, while Wyoming and Idaho remained territories, raised a furor which brought statehood in 1890 for those two areas as well. Utah, Arizona, and New Mexico still retained territorial status, and in 1890 Congress created Oklahoma Territory, comprising only part of the present-day state. Indian tribal holdings made up the rest of that area.

Population by 1890 had increased another 12,700,000. This 25 per cent increase, while slower growth than in previous decades, brought total population to more than 62,900,000. In the East population pressure on the land resulted in a shrinking of unsettled areas in Maine and Florida as well as in the Adirondack area of New York. Michigan's unsettled area disappeared and vacant timber areas in northern Wisconsin diminished. Partly as a result of efforts of western railroad companies to populate land grants along their routes, the biggest push of settlement was into the unsettled West. Settlers surged far into the Dakotas and pushed far enough west in Kansas and Nebraska to merge with eastward moving settlements in Colorado and Wyoming. New Mexico settlement stretched into western Texas, while east Texas settlements continued to expand toward the west. A substantial settled area also sprang up in newly opened Oklahoma Territory. Settlements in South Dakota that developed with the gold rush to the Black Hills expanded greatly. Growing population connected isolated settlements and extended along river valleys through much of Montana and the Northwest. Settlers occupied much of Idaho, but nearly complete utilization of irrigable lands limited expansion in Utah. Settlements in Nevada and Arizona exhibited only slight expansion. Some filling in of Pacific coast areas took place, and settlement grew greatly along the Idaho border in eastern Washington. Together with the continued expansion of older settled areas, new islands of settlement sprang up in most plains and mountain states. Rapid land occupation in the West brought a great increase in land offices from 96 to 122 in this decade. These offices were concentrated west of the Mississippi River, with one opened in Alaska. Nebraska alone had twelve, Colorado, thirteen, and even Oklahoma Territory had four land offices. Only eleven remained east of the Mississippi.

The filling in of vacant areas, and the connection of western settlements to the Middlewest and to one another, prompted the Director of the United States Census Bureau to announce that, while in 1880 it had still been possible to draw a "frontier line," by 1890 the unsettled areas had been so broken up that this was no longer possible. In 1893 Frederick Jackson Turner, then a young Wisconsin historian, seized on this announcement to enunciate a theory of American development based on westward expansion. Turner became the best-known historian of the West, and his hypothesis that the westward movement was responsible for a unique American character served as the stimulus for much of the study of American continental expansion. It is possible, however, that the disappearance of the frontier which inspired Turner was less the result of population growth than of imaginative cartography. The map of 1890 population distribution prepared by the Bureau connected isolated settlements with bands of population along river valleys which, while they may have a certain logic, may not in fact have existed. At any rate the cartographer in preparing the 1900 map found no such connections, although population had not receded but grown.

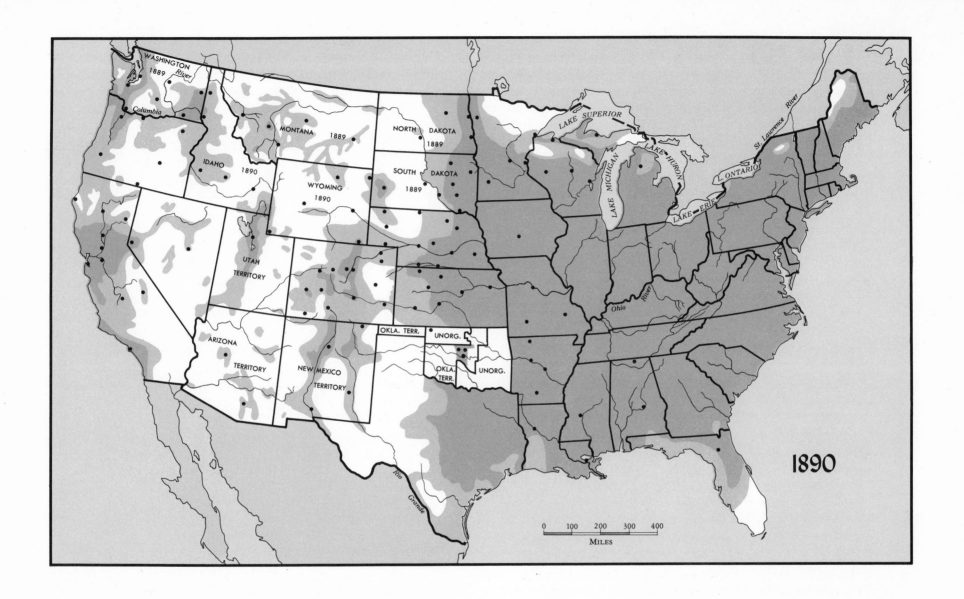

1890

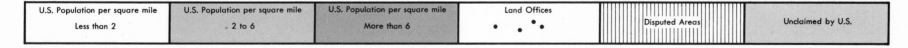

1900

By 1900 Americans had largely completed the process of occupying the continent and the Bureau of the Census had officially announced the disappearance of the frontier. In 1896 Utah, long kept out of the Union by anti-Mormon sentiment, became a state, but the other territories remained. Oklahoma Territory, which in 1900 still comprised only part of the present state, entered the Union in 1907. Arizona and New Mexico Territories, confined within their final borders for many years, did not achieve statehood until 1912. They became the forty-seventh and forty-eighth of the states which made up the United States until 1959 and 1960 when the noncontiguous territories, Alaska and Hawaii, became states as well.

In the last decade of the nineteenth century, population continued its enormous growth, if at a somewhat slower rate. By 1900 there were thirteen million more people in the United States than ten years before, an increase of only 21 per cent. The new population added in this decade, however, was nearly four times the total population in 1790 at the first census, and it brought the total to more than 76,300,000 people. In 1900 the distribution of population across the nation differed from 1890 in an unusual way. Although the Adirondack area in New York and the forest area of northern Wisconsin had filled in, almost no significant changes took place east of the Mississippi. The most striking advance of settlement was the almost complete occupation of long-vacant Oklahoma when lands there became subject to settlement. The characteristic feature of the 1900 distribution, however, was not advance but retreat. Apparent pulling back of settlement in the plains disconnected Kansas and Nebraska settlements from those in the western plains and foothills. Connected settlement in Arizona, Nevada, and eastern Montana also broke into a series of isolated settlements, while the eastward advance from the Pacific coast stopped or retreated. Only in western Montana and eastern Utah was any growth or consolidation apparent. The characteristic "frontier line," which disappeared in 1890, reap-

peared very clearly in 1900 as settlements, connected ten years before, separated. Since in all the states where connecting settlements disappeared population showed continued growth rather than recession, it is possible that the differences in population distribution between the 1890 map and those for 1880 and 1900 resulted from differences in cartographic generalization rather than in the settlement pattern. Land occupation continued unabated, and as public lands diminished, the number of land offices dropped for the first time. Total land offices fell from 122 to 117 between 1890 and 1900, but activity continued to concentrate in the West. Only nine offices remained east of the Mississippi, while Alaska alone had three.

By 1900 not one but five major railroad systems traversed the trans-Mississippi West to the Pacific. By 1895 the most northerly of these, James J. Hill's Great Northern Railroad, stretched from St. Paul to Seattle. Hill built his line without significant land grants or federal subsidies. Slightly to the south lay the Northern Pacific Railroad, chartered in 1864 with the aid of a land grant and subsidies. By 1884 it connected both Duluth and St. Paul with Portland and Tacoma. The Union Pacific-Central Pacific line, already connecting Omaha with Sacramento by 1869, in 1881 opened the Oregon Shortline. This branch of the mainline swung north in Wyoming and connected the system to Huntington, Oregon on the Snake River. The Atchison, Topeka and Santa Fe Railroad, by consolidating several smaller lines, by 1885 built a system that connected Atchison, Kansas with the Pacific coast. The Southern Pacific Railroad was the most southerly route. By 1884, aided by land grants and subsidies, it built new track and connected several small railroads to form a single line from New Orleans to the Pacific along the Gila River route. By 1900 these lines, with their numerous branches and subsidiaries, provided an elaborate network of rail facilities connecting the settlements of the West with their main sources of population and capital to the east.

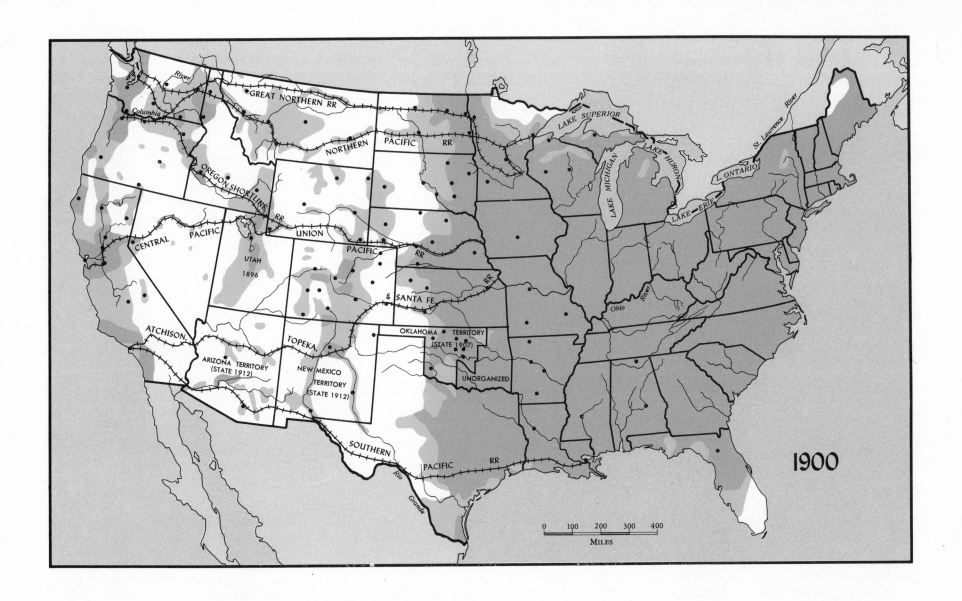

GREAT NORTHERN RR

NORTHERN PACIFIC RR

OREGON SHORTLINE RR

CENTRAL PACIFIC

UNION PACIFIC RR

UTAH 1896

& SANTA FE

ATCHISON,

TOPEKA,

ARIZONA TERRITORY (STATE 1912)

NEW MEXICO TERRITORY (STATE 1912)

OKLAHOMA TERRITORY (STATE 1907)

UNORGANIZED

SOUTHERN PACIFIC RR

River

Columbia

Rio Grande

Ohio River

LAKE SUPERIOR

LAKE MICHIGAN

LAKE HURON

LAKE ERIE

L. ONTARIO

St. Lawrence River

1900

0   100   200   300   400
MILES

| U.S. Population per square mile Less than 2 | U.S. Population per square mile 2 to 6 | U.S. Population per square mile More than 6 | Land Offices | Disputed Areas | Unclaimed by U.S. |

LAND OFFICES

1790

New York
New York

1800

Northwest Territory
Chillicothe
Cincinnati
Marietta
Steubenville

1810

Ohio
Canton
Chillicothe
Cincinnati
Marietta
Steubenville
Zanesville
Indiana Territory
Jefferson
Vincennes
Mississippi Territory
Huntsville
St. Stephens
Washington

1820

Alabama
Cahaba
Conecuh C. H.
Huntsville
St. Stephens
Tuscaloosa
Illinois
Edwardsville
Kaskaskia
Palestine
Shawneetown
Vandalia

Indiana
Brookville
Jeffersonville
Terre Haute
Vincennes
Louisiana
New Orleans
Opelousas
Ouachita
St. Helena C. H.
Mississippi
Jackson
Washington
Ohio
Chillicothe
Cincinnati
Delaware
Marietta
Piqua
Steubenville
Wooster
Zanesville
Arkansas Territory
Little Rock
Polk Bayou
Michigan Territory
Detroit
Missouri Territory
Cape Girardeau
Franklin
St. Louis

1830

Alabama
Cahaba
Huntsville
St. Stephens
Sparta
Tuscaloosa
Illinois
Edwardsville
Kaskaskia

Palestine
Shawneetown
Springfield
Vandalia
Indiana
Crawfordsville
Fort Wayne
Indianapolis
Jeffersonville
Vincennes
Louisiana
Helena
New Orleans
Opelousas
Ouachita
Mississippi
Augusta
Mount Salus
Washington
Missouri
Franklin
Jackson
Lexington
Palmyra
St. Louis
Ohio
Chillicothe
Cincinnati
Marietta
Piqua
Steubenville
Tiffin
Wooster
Zanesville
Arkansas Territory
Batesville
Little Rock
Florida Territory
St. Augustine
Tallahassee
Michigan Territory
Detroit
Monroe

1840

Alabama
Cahaba
Demopolis
Huntsville
Mardisville
Montgomery
St. Stephens
Sparta
Tuscaloosa
Arkansas
Batesville
Fayetteville
Helena
Johnson C. H.
Little Rock
Washington
Illinois
Chicago
Danville
Edwardsville
Galena
Kaskaskia
Palestine
Quincy
Shawneetown
Springfield
Vandalia
Indiana
Crawfordsville
Fort Wayne
Indianapolis
Jeffersonville
Vincennes
Winamac
Louisiana
Greenburg
Natchitoches
New Orleans
Opelousas
Ouachita
Michigan
Detroit
Genesee
Ionia
Kalamazoo

Monroe
Mississippi
Augusta
Columbus
Grenada
Jackson
Washington
Missouri
Fayette
Jackson
Lexington
Palmyra
St. Louis
Springfield
Ohio
Bucyrus
Chillicothe
Cincinnati
Lima
Marietta
Steubenville
Wooster
Zanesville
Florida Territory
St. Augustine
Tallahassee
Iowa Territory
Burlington
Dubuque
Wisconsin Territory
Green Bay
Milwaukee
Mineral Point

1850

Alabama
Cahaba
Demopolis
Huntsville
Lebanon
Montgomery
St. Stephens
Sparta

Tuscaloosa
Arkansas
Batesville
Champagnole
Clarksville
Fayetteville
Helena
Little Rock
Washington
Florida
Newnansville
St. Augustine
Tallahassee
Illinois
Chicago
Danville
Dixon
Edwardsville
Kaskaskia
Palestine
Quincy
Shawneetown
Springfield
Vandalia
Indiana
Crawfordsville
Fort Wayne
Indianapolis
Jeffersonville
Vincennes
Winamac
Iowa
Dubuque
Fairfield
Iowa City
Louisiana
Greenburg
Monroe
Natchitoches
New Orleans
Opelousas
Michigan
Detroit
Genesee
Ionia
Kalamazoo
Sault Ste. Marie

Mississippi
Augusta
Columbus
Grenada
Jackson
Washington
Missouri
Clinton
Fayette
Jackson
Milan
Palmyra
Plattsburg
St. Louis
Springfield
Ohio
Chillicothe
Defiance
Wisconsin
Green Bay
Milwaukee
Mineral Point
Willow River
Minnesota Territory
Stillwater

1860

Alabama
Centre
Demopolis
Elba
Greenville
Huntsville
Montgomery
St. Stephens
Tuscaloosa
Arkansas
Batesville
Champagnole
Clarksville
Huntsville
Little Rock
Washington
California
Humboldt

Los Angeles
Marysville
San Francisco
Stockton
Visalia
Florida
Newnansville
St. Augustine
Tallahassee
Tampa
Illinois
Springfield
Indiana
~~Indianapolis~~

Council Bluffs
Ft. Des Moines
Fort Dodge
Sioux City
Louisiana
Greenburg
Monroe
Natchitoches
New Orleans
Opelousas
Michigan
Detroit
East Saginaw
Ionia
Marquette
Traverse City
Minnesota
Chatfield
Forest City
Henderson
Otter Tail City
Portland
St. Cloud
St. Peter
Sunrise City
Mississippi
Columbus
Grenada
Jackson
Pauldin
Washington

Missouri
Boonville
Jackson
St. Louis
Springfield
Warsaw
Ohio
Chillicothe
Oregon
Oregon City
Roseberg
Wisconsin
Bayfield
Eau Claire
La Crosse
Menasha
St. Croix Falls
Stevens Point
Kansas
Territory
Fort Scott
Junction City
Lecompton
Kickapoo
Nebraska
Territory
Brownville
Dakota City
Nebraska City
Omaha City
New Mexico
Territory
Santa Fe
Washington
Territory
Olympia

1870

Alabama
Huntsville
Mobile
Montgomery
Arkansas
Camden
Clarksville
Dardanelle

Harrison
Little Rock
Washington
California
Humboldt
Los Angeles
Marysville
Sacramento
San Francisco
Shasta
Stockton
Susanville
Visalia
Florida
Tallahassee
Illinois
Springfield
Indiana
Indianapolis
Iowa
Council Bluffs
Ft. Des Moines
Fort Dodge
Sioux City
Kansas
Augusta
Concordia
Humboldt
Junction City
Salina
Topeka
Louisiana
Monroe
Natchitoches
New Orleans
Michigan
Detroit
East Saginaw
Ionia
Marquette
Traverse City
Minnesota
Alexandria
Duluth
Jackson
Litchfield
New Ulm

St. Cloud
Taylors Falls
Mississippi
Jackson
Missouri
Boonville
Ironton
Springfield
Nebraska
Beatrice
Dakota City
Grand Island
Lincoln
West Point
Nevada
Austin

Idaho
Territory
Boise City
Lewiston
Montana
Territory
Helena
New Mexico
Territory
Santa Fe
Utah
Territory
Salt Lake City
Washington
Territory
Olympia

Leadville
Pueblo
Florida
Gainesville
Iowa
Des Moines
Kansas
Concordia
Independence
Kirwin
Larned
Salina
Topeka
Wakeeney
Wichita
Louisiana
Natchitoches
New Orleans
Michigan
Detroit
Saginaw
Marquette
Reed City
Minnesota
Benson
Jackson
Falls
Redwood Falls
St. Cloud
Taylors Falls
Mississippi
Jackson
Missouri
ville
on
Springfield
Nebraska
rice
Bloomington
Grand Island
Lincoln
Niobrara
Norfolk
North Platte

Nevada
Carson City
Eureka
Oregon
La Grande
Lakeview
Oregon City
Roseberg
The Dalles
Wisconsin
Bayfield
Eau Claire
La Crosse
Menasha
St. Croix Falls
Wausau
Arizona
Territory
Florence
Prescott
Dakota
Territory
Bismarck
Deadwood
Fargo
Grand Forks
Mitchell
Watertown
Yankton
Idaho
Territory
Boise City
Lewiston
Oxford
Montana
Territory
Bozeman
Helena
Miles City
New Mexico
Territory
La Mesilla
Santa Fe

*Continued on
Back Cover*

27

LAND OFFICES (Cont'd)

Utah
Territory
Salt Lake City
Washington
Territory
Colfax
Olympia
Vancouver
Walla Walla
Yakima
Wyoming
Territory
Cheyenne
Evanston

1890

Alabama
Huntsville
Montgomery
Arkansas
Camden
Dardanelle
Harrison
Little Rock
California
Humboldt
Independence
Los Angeles
Marysville
Redding
Sacramento
San Francisco
Stockton
Susanville
Visalia
Colorado
Akron
Central City
Del Norte
Denver
Durango
Glenwood Springs
Gunnison
Hugo
Lamar

Leadville
Montrose
Pueblo
Sterling
Florida
Gainesville
Idaho
Blackfoot
Boise City
Coeur d'Alene
Hailey
Lewiston
Iowa
Des Moines
Kansas
Garden City
Kirwin
Larned
Oberlin
Salina
Topeka
Wakeeney
Louisiana
Natchitoches
New Orleans
Michigan
Grayling
Marquette
Minnesota
Crookston
Duluth
Marshall
St. Cloud
Taylors Falls
Mississippi
Jackson
Missouri
Boonville
Ironton
Springfield
Montana
Bozeman
Helena
Lewiston
Miles City
Missoula

Nebraska
Alliance
Bloomington
Broken Bow
Chadron
Grand Island
Lincoln
McCook
Neligh
North Platte
O'Neill
Sidney
Valentine
Nevada
Carson City
Eureka
North Dakota
Bismarck
Devils Lake
Fargo
Grand Forks
Oregon
Burns
La Grande
Lakeview
Oregon City
Roseberg
The Dalles
South Dakota
Aberdeen
Chamberlain
Huron
Mitchell
Pierre
Rapid City
Watertown
Yankton
Washington
North Yakima
Olympia
Seattle
Spokane Falls
Vancouver
Walla Walla
Waterville
Wisconsin

Ashland
Eau Claire
Menasha
Wausau
Wyoming
Buffalo
Cheyenne
Douglas
Evanston
Lander
Sundance
Arizona
Territory
Prescott
Tucson
New Mexico
Territory
Folsom
Las Cruces
Roswell
Santa Fe
Oklahoma
Territory
Buffalo
Guthrie
Kingfisher
Oklahoma City
Utah
Territory
Salt Lake City
Alaska
Territory
Sitka

1900

Alabama
Huntsville
Montgomery
Arkansas
Camden
Dardanelle
Harrison
Little Rock
California
Eureka

Independence
Los Angeles
Marysville
Redding
Sacramento
San Francisco
Stockton
Susanville
Visalia
Colorado
Akron
Del Norte
Denver
Durango
Glenwood Springs
Gunnison
Hugo
Lamar
Leadville
Montrose
Pueblo
Sterling
Florida
Gainesville
Idaho
Blackfoot
Boise
Coeur d'Alene
Hailey
Lewiston
Iowa
Des Moines
Kansas
Colby
Dodge City
Topeka
Wakeeney
Louisiana
Natchitoches
New Orleans
Michigan
Marquette
Minnesota
Crookston
Duluth
Marshall

St. Cloud
Mississippi
Jackson
Missouri
Boonville
Ironton
Springfield
Montana
Bozeman
Helena
Kalispell
Lewiston
Miles City
Missoula
Nebraska
Alliance
Broken Bow
Lincoln
McCook
North Platte
O'Neill
Sidney
Valentine
Nevada
Carson City
North Dakota
Bismarck
Devils Lake
Fargo
Grand Forks
Minot
Oregon
Burns
La Grande
Lakeview
Oregon City
Roseberg
The Dalles
South Dakota
Aberdeen
Chamberlain
Huron
Mitchell
Pierre
Rapid City
Watertown

Utah
Salt Lake City
Washington
North Yakima
Olympia
Seattle
Spokane
Vancouver
Walla Walla
Waterville
Wisconsin
Ashland
Eau Claire
Wausau
Wyoming
Buffalo
Cheyenne
Douglas
Evanston
Lander
Sundance
Arizona
Territory
Prescott
Tucson
New Mexico
Territory
Clayton
Las Cruces
Roswell
Santa Fe
Oklahoma
Territory
Alva
Enid
Guthrie
Kingfisher
Mangum
Oklahoma City
Perry
Woodward
Alaska
Territory
Rampart City
St. Michael
Sit...